How to
s

GW01464138

Your w... is ... my hands.

Non-Fiction

By: Ina Stein

1st Edition 2005

© Copyright by Carl Stephenson Verlag,
Schäferweg 14, D-24941 Flensburg
All rights reserved including storage and processing
on electronic media.
e-mail: info@stephenson.de
Internet: www.stephenson.de
Print: Nørhaven Paperback, DK-8800 Viborg
Printed in Denmark

ISBN 3-7986-0182-8
0130362 0000 • 96 pages

How to dominate HER sexually

Your will is in my hands!

Non-Fiction

By: Ina Stein

Table of Contents:

Being free means
being able to choose
whose slave you want to be.

Jeanne Moreau
(Actress)

Preface

Eroticism comprises countless predilections and varieties a *normally inclined* person will never experience. Anything going beyond the *normal* in sex is seen as kinky. „*I could never imagine that — that's just perverse!*" many of those who hear about BD/SM (bondage and discipline, dominance and submission, S/M) for the first time will say; whether S/M, latex and leather fetishism or voyeurism, bondage, caning or another erotic variety: one is shocked!

At least many claim to be disgusted. But if we're honest we have to admit that everything going beyond the normal also holds a strange attraction for many of us. It excites us though we don't want to admit it. Inside we sit up and take notice, and images spring up in our mind's eye that make us feel ashamed and shocked on the one hand, but excited on the other hand. They put us off balance, for we have been brought up to act and react *normally* — also as far as sex is concerned. But isn't it precisely the wicked, the forbidden, the social taboos we find tempting? Wouldn't many just love to throw off the shackles of social conventions tying them down to finally act out their sexual fantasies? For these aren't always *normal* — thank God!

Unfortunately only a few people dare to cross that threshold because their upbringing has instilled them with shame and fear at the thought of it. Instead of acting out our own erotic fantasies and abandoning ourselves to our sexual inclinations, we lock up these dreams in the darkest recesses of our ego, incarcerate them and thus condemn ourselves to a life of sexual dissatisfaction. One thing is sure, though: once these desires — no matter what kind — exist, we can't pretend forever that they don't. That approach is wrong and will surely make us discontented.

There's a battle raging inside of us, and though we would like to ignore it, we can't. These desires exert an enormous power, paralyse a large part of our psyche and can't be turned off just like that. On the contrary — we should see our sexual desires and fantasies as an enrichment of our sex life, check out our proclivities and have fun approaching the matter together with our partner!

Granted, that's not that easy. Especially in a relationship — no matter if partnership or marriage — both partners should be quite cautious in dealing with the subject of sexuality, whereas caution shouldn't be confused with being uptight. Because the subject of eroticism shouldn't be devoid of ease, openness and above all humour! Here, caution means above all showing consideration for the wishes and sexual limits of the other, respecting the other's anxieties and needs and handling the other's body and soul with love. To jointly explore something previously unknown, to enjoy new feelings while at the same time never losing track of the partner's psychological and physical limits, that's the mark of a true and therefore happy partnership.

The relationship between two people is something unique — not just in terms of sex. It is an extremely complex network, intertwined and very delicate, yet also very stress-resistant. That's especially true once dominance is brought into play. It heightens sensibilities in a partnership, because even seemingly unimportant actions and certain gestures and words are suddenly appreciated much more and gradually develop into special rituals or become part of these. Often, the words or gestures are completely inconspicuous to outsiders; they mean a whole lot to both partners, though: they are a big and very important part of their lives, a part they no longer want to do without. Because once you have discovered this special inclination in yourself — be it one of dominance or submission — and tried out games of this kind, the experience of the sensual appeal and sexual satisfaction won't let go of you. For both partners it is like a sweet, *forbidden* craving ...

But first, the first step must be taken — and that's the hardest, as everyone knows. For most people it is basically quite hard to confess their special sexual desires to their partners. To put it in more concrete terms, many men ask themselves (and this is the what we're dealing with in this book): *„How do I get her to fulfil my sexual desires without destroying our partnership?"* These desires could be oral sex or bondage games, but also anal sex, nappy fetish, outdoor sex or caning. What are the possibilities of telling her your own desires and acting them out with her? How do you make your partner *compliant* and let her overcome her own taboos so that she will eventually notice how delightful these erotic varieties can be?

As our examples will show, a little *voluntary coercion* is initially an important prerequisite to allow the partner to justify herself. For the fact that she is more or less forced to commit certain sexual acts or submit to these allows her to have a clear conscience and remain innocent as far as her moral conceptions are concerned. It's not she who broke this taboo. After all, she was forced by her partner; the fact that she enjoyed it and that she experienced great sexual satisfaction, then, is a *side effect*, as it were …

As our firsthand reports will show, chance often comes to the aid, that is the first act of BD/SM often grows out of a special, though unplanned, situation. The first careful step is taken, testing the partner's reaction, and if she is responsive to this, there won't be any limit to the imagination in future. The BD/SM rituals become ever more polished, and the entire relationship gains a whole new dimension.

How two people are living together and if both perceive the subject of authority at the same *level*, can vary widely; there are many variations in this area, ranging from equality between both partners or slight sexual dominance and harder or actual dominance up to complete submission and extreme sadomasochism. The relationship to each other may change in the course of a partnership, the scales of authority can tip to one side, for example if over time the desire for stricter leadership grows ever stronger in one partner or the striving for power becomes ever more pronounced in the other.

By the way, these inclinations don't just extend to the erotic area of a partnership. Often the boundaries will blur and partly spill over into everyday life, as the reports of our interviewees will show. One thing became quite clear in these talks: BD/SM can be very exciting and enriching. It is titillating beyond words and ideally offers both partners a whole new dimension of feelings and above all absolute sexual satisfaction. It is downright addictive and can therefore become a philosophy of life. But it is also a dangerous game that requires just the right touch and respect for the partner's state of mind.

The objective of our research was to find out how BD/SM can concretely take its course in a partnership, how these rituals evolve in the first place, if they are there from the beginning or if they are slowly discovered and developed. For example, we want people who have some experience in this area to tell us:

- *What accounts for the appeal of this erotic variety, this philosophy of life?*
- *What makes your partnership different from others?*
- *In what do you find your sexual and spiritual fulfilment?*
- *How can such a special relationship develop?*
- *How can sexual desires be fulfilled through dominance in the partnership?*
- *How do BD/SM rituals evolve?*
- *How does it differ from other sexual practices?*

Our interviewees answered these and many other questions quite openly by simply describing special erotic circumstances in their partnership. Their reports give an insight into those partnerships in which the game of power and submission has become an indispensable part living together. We want to show in concrete terms what such a bizarre partnership can look like, and above all we want this book to be seen as a call for more understanding towards people with a penchant for S/M practices. They are not *perverse*, just *different*; they set themselves apart from the normal and in doing so bestow great happiness on themselves and their partner: absolute physical and emotional satisfaction.

At the same time we want to sway those who feel they have a weakness for this erotic variety, but are afraid to act on these feelings and therefore feel insecure, to turn the seemingly negative into something positive: talk to your partner about it or give her small hints at first; check out her desires and yours, let your fantasy become reality!

Live out your sexual predilections instead of letting your relationship **die** because you're stifling your longings. Allow small rituals to enter your relationship, experiment together with your partner. Dominance and submission, punishment and obedience are terms that deter many of us; for others, however, they mean heaven on earth.

Ina Stein

The Allure of Power and Submission

It's all in your head

Eroticism primarily takes place in our heads. While sexuality seems to be a purely physical act at first glance, those who examine it a little closer soon notice that the origin of each sexual action is in our heads. It is our thoughts, feelings, certain fantasies, ideas and desires that set off each erotic session we experience. These thoughts, however, are often triggered by outside sensory perceptions like the sight of an attractive partner or an erotic photo, the smell of a scent that is perceived as sensual or the sound of romantic music. So the desire in our heads can be triggered by outside stimuli, after which our fantasy begins to work until we finally start to act. In front of our inner eye we are already experiencing sexual scenes long before acting these out in reality — and that excites us! We already feel eroticism long before it comes to a sexual act — and that's an enormous turn-on!

Of course people experience these processes with varying degrees of intensity. To give you an example of both extremes: while one person may not care what's happening inside his head, deliberately suppressing or not wanting to enjoy these erotic fantasies or not even noticing them in the first place, another person may savour them to the last, wallowing very often and for a long time in these erotic dream worlds — even to the point where they possibly replace reality; these fantasies are then enough for this person to reach sexual satisfaction. These are two extreme cases, of course, and can't be considered the norm.

A *happy medium* are those people who have an erotic idea, wish or fantasy in their heads and deliberately hold and enjoy it there for a while — like the bouquet of a good wine — while looking forward to its realization. Our ability to imagine things may add further images to these fantasies. Our sexual arousal is therefore triggered by the *cinema in our head* and continues to grow until the focus shifts from our head to physical action.

The allure of power also begins in the head. It's like a drug you can't get enough of. It lets you take wing, fills you with strength and energy. Everyone who has experienced this high knows what I mean. The allure of power is ancient and can be found tempting us in almost all areas of life — not just in our sexuality. Of course we are familiar with power from politics, where it has shaped the lives of people since time immemorial. And from our professional life we know the extreme of the *power-hungry* manager. It's no coincidence that companies are structured in hierarchies where superiors give instructions to subordinate employees and check on their work. Normally, though, the duties and responsibilities of those exercising power also increase with the level of power they hold. This is also true for exercising power in sexuality. But more on this later.

Whatever kind of power you are looking at: power holds a very special thrill for many people and is therefore very desirable. To have someone at your disposal is extremely tempting — and can also be sexually stimulating! On a biological level, this stimulation is caused by a quick and inordinate surge of adrenaline, a hormone that mobilizes your metabolism in situations of danger and stress. The basal metabolic rate, blood sugar level, blood supply to muscles and coronary arteries as well as the output of the heart are all increased. It feels like getting an enormous surge in energy! And the longer and more intensely you have been looking forward to it, the longer you have been fantasizing about it, the more you will enjoy this feeling of power!

What makes sexual dominance so tempting is that one partner is doing what the other wants. This dependency can be underscored through bondage or flogging games or even through *torture*. The first priority is to give yourself and the dominated partner the greatest possible pleasure with all sexual acts. The decision as to when and how lies exclusively with the holder of power. He is the active one, the one in control, in short, the ruler!

However, prerequisite for all sexual power games is trust. Someone who loves his partner will never cross certain boundaries that both have established together. While he may exert a certain level of pressure and force, for that is part of the dominance game, he will never force his partner to do anything she really doesn't want to. Of course, part of the attraction of power is to steer the will of the partner, to control and be the dominant force when making love. However, the dominant partner will never really take unscrupulous advantage of his sexual power. Because the submissive partner must give her consent to all sexual practices the dominant partner desires — be it through words, looks or gestures. She therefore deliberately takes on the position of the powerless, which is actually a paradox, that is a contradiction in itself. For if you can choose to be powerless, you are not really powerless. But the submissive partner must make that decision before she submits to the will of the other. It is her last self-determined act, so to speak, before entering dependency. Only if the submissive partner approves of this game (either through words, gestures or obvious action or non-action) beforehand can there be a guarantee that she is doing it voluntarily and that the psychological and physical subjugation is not an offence.

While this book deals with the most common role play of *dominant man — submissive woman*, we would still like to note at this point that there are also cases where the opposite is true. Therefore, when it comes to erotic power games it is not always only men who find pleasure in this game and who want to control their partner. It happens that those men who in their professional or family life have to be especially strong and constantly have to show they're in control or have all the answers want nothing more than to finally have someone else decide for them in their sex life. They're all too happy to hand over the heavy burden of power and responsibility to experience the other side for a change. At long last they don't have to make any decisions and can simply enjoy the fantasy of the active, powerful partner and the thrill of not knowing what's going to happen next. Often, bondage games come into play so that physical power is exercised, too. The tied-up partner is defenceless! Basically one can say: whoever masters his daily life with strength and self-determination doesn't mind letting go and be led in his sex life now and then — no matter if man or woman!

Conversely, people who in *normal* life are rather reserved can rid themselves of shyness and submission through sexual dominance (though this happens much less frequently). Here they gain the experience that sexuality doesn't always have to be something passive, that one should take over the reins now and then — in the true sense of the word!

But as I said: that rarely happens. In most cases in which sexual dominance is an important factor in the partnership, it is the men who are dominating their partners — and the women who are quite consciously going along with this role!

Experiences of Torment and Lust

Firsthand Reports: First I forced her, then she cried for more ...

How it all started? For many of our interviewees it wasn't easy answering that question, because BD/SM doesn't start from one day to the next. Most often the male desire for dominance or the female desire for submission has already been there in a relationship for quite some time. The inclination is there, only living it out is still a problem because the partners don't have the courage to tell each other their secret desires.

You ask yourself: *„How can I communicate with my partner about the subject of sexuality?"* On the one hand there is reality, on the other hand there are our fantasies and wishes we would like to see fulfilled to experience a satisfying sexuality. Many men ask themselves: *„How can I talk to her about it without hurting her? How can I help her understand my secret wishes?"* In the end, many give up because they are afraid to make a mistake ...

But keeping it inside and suppressing it would be wrong, because in doing so we aren't giving ourselves — and our partner! — the chance to experience something that could enrich our life together and make us happier. There are ways and means for every man to overcome this barrier and to take his partner to a point where she will satisfy his (and in the end also her own!) most secret wishes — at first possibly under a certain pressure, but later all on her own because she finally will have come to like this erotic game of being punished very much!

In numerous interviews men and women of all ages and different social backgrounds talk about their very personal experiences with the allure of BD/SM. Understandably, they were only willing to divulge their experiences to the public anonymously. Basically it doesn't matter at all who they are, where they live and what they do for a living. We just let them talk, listened to them and showed interest and understanding for this very special kind of erotic life together. Our interviews resulted in erotic stories of a very special kind, where one often has to read between the lines ...

What our interviewees disclosed are stories that reflect the entire range of this special sexual variety. They range from the beginnings of sexual dominance within a partnership via deliberate male power games and humiliation in public to planned meetings of like-minded people, in which the woman lets herself be shown off. This erotic proclivity of two partners is nevertheless different from pure sadomasochism, though one can see certain parallels here and there. As with so much in sexuality, the boundaries may be blurred here, too.

Here, now, are the firsthand reports of our BD/SM fans that will give the attentive reader an interesting look into the beguiling world of this special sexual inclination:

The Ritual

Sylvia from F. (35): Maybe it sounds a little weird, but the strange thing was that the rest of our relationship was completely normal. Outside the bed we were equal partners. We talked about our common interests, went to the cinema, the museum or the park. He cooked for me and I for him. We were a normal couple. But one day, in the middle of a conversation, Albert asked me:

„*What can you do for me, slave?*" — The effect was like magic!

A little later I was lying naked at his feet, indulging him. He bound and gagged me and did with me whatever he thought of at the moment. And I was happy — wonderfully happy!

Albert respected me in two ways: as an intellectual, intelligent woman and as slave to our lust. With him I learned to be both without coming into conflict with myself. He showed me how to live out my sexuality without any reservations. He opened up new worlds of pleasure to me, respected me as a woman and loved me as his slave. Perverse? Crazy? — Why? After all, the two of us had fun, and that's all that counts!

I used to be different. I was uptight and ashamed about my erotic desires and fantasies. While Albert had a hunch that I shared these fantasies, he also knew that I would never divulge these to him on my own. My strict upbringing made that impossible; my parents had drummed certain moral concepts into me — and there was no room for wild ecstasy and bizarre, *perverse* little games like anal sex and caning! I was a prisoner of my inhibitions and would never have been able to get rid of these on my own ...

Albert knew there was only one way for me to abandon myself to my sexual desires and break all taboos: he had to give me the chance of not having to justify myself to myself; he had to force me! Only then would I be able to act freely and to open up all my erotic fantasies. And today it's exactly like that: The moment he suddenly starts our ritual — out of the blue — with that certain sentence, I can hand over my responsibility and put myself in his hands completely.

„*What can you do for me, slave?*" My God, how I love these words! They are my fulfilment ...

Absolute Sexual Obedience

Frank from D. (40): Absolute sexual obedience — for me a term that carries a huge potential in erotic magnetism! I can't change the fact that I'm an avowed BD/SM fan, because the ever new game of power and submission gives my sex life an especially exciting flair that I can't find anywhere else. It gives me and my wife a special kick of pleasure!

But it wasn't always like that. First I had to slowly introduce her to this variety of sex and teach her the rules. Basically, though, it's not me who is doing that, but I'm just helping her to discover her own potential, to uncover and enjoy it! I only showed her what had been inside of her for a long time anyway: the road to absolute pleasure!

You want to hear an example how these rituals go with us? Very well:

„*Put on your coat, Gina, only the long, black one. I want to test your absolute obedience.*"

My command comes out of the blue, and I don't say

anything more. She walks to the closet and reaches for her coat to put it on.

„*Did I say anything about any other clothes, Gina? No. I said ONLY the coat.*"

She hesitates a moment and then takes off her pants, blouse and underwear where she stands, letting her things drop to the floor. Before she rolls down her lace-fringed, strapless silk stockings and slips out of her high-heeled pumps, she gives me another questioning look.

„*That's okay, you can keep those on.*"

Gina throws the coat over her body and waits patiently. Our special ritual has begun, the stimulating fantasies in her head begin to unwind, because she knows that something lustful is waiting for her – she just doesn't know what it might be today!

I lead her to the car and let her get in. It is a cold, late afternoon on a grey day in February. I start driving without another word. The mysterious sound of *Gregorian Chants* are emanating from the speakers, underscoring the special mood, the highly erotic tension between the two of us.

I've never been to the place where I want to go now. A friend has told me about this special place, where extremely exciting experiences are waiting for us, so I hope …

It takes about half an hour to get to the secluded, dark parking lot. Gina still doesn't know what's in store for her today. As soon as I have parked the car – there are no other cars close by, but there are about ten cars some distance away – I turn off the engine and turn down the music a little. Now the dark sounds only provide a musical background without being the focus of attention. That will be something quite different soon: Gina's absolute sexual obedience!

I peel the coat off her shoulders, throw it on the back seat and at the same time pick up the foot bar I had hidden there: an iron bar, about 80 centimetres long, that has a leather cuff fixed to each end. Gina willingly spreads her legs and lets the bar be attached to her ankles. Now she can't close her legs anymore, the bar forcing her to keep her thighs spread. Her genitals and the rest of her body are without protection.

„Put your arms behind you!“, my voice cuts into the silence, and Gina obeys. She bends backwards a little and I tie her hands to each other with a long rope behind the backrest of the passenger seat. While she doesn't feel any pain because the rope is long enough and not bound all too tightly, she is still forced to push out her breasts and no longer can put her arms in front of her. I like my work. I smile at her and get out of the car.

„Where are you going — what am I supposed to do here all alone?“, I hear her ask anxiously as I walk slowly away into the darkness.

I have hardly walked a ways towards the parked cars when I can already see a few figures standing there. Some are smoking, others are talking quietly, but most of them are standing there alone as if they were waiting for something.

As soon as I am within earshot, I call out to them: *„That woman there in the car — she's yours, go take a look at her!“*

The men (I guess there were about ten or twelve) immediately flock in the direction of my car. I follow them, because I don't want to miss the expression on Gina's face when she sees the strangers.

The men, whose faces can hardly be recognized in the dark, surround the car and stare at the passenger seat. They are turned on by Gina's nakedness and helplessness and press their lecherous faces against the windows. I can read fear in Gina's eyes.

Some men begin to moan and utter excited sounds. There is a general buzz from which I can filter out fragments like *whore*, *easy bitch* and *touch*. Some of the men even open their pants now ...

Suddenly I have an idea. „*You want to touch her?*", I ask those present, and all approve enthusiastically. I know they won't be allowed to go any further, that there are certain rules and predetermined boundaries at this special place that's so exciting — but Gina doesn't know it! So I open the car door and my beauty stares at me in horror — horrified and wonderfully aroused!

Then I step back and take position in front of the car so that I can see everything. One after the other the men step up to the passenger seat next to Gina and touch her. Some of them unerringly grab between her thighs, others massage her breasts while still another one attends to her nipples. All of them have to say something about it, call her names and fill her ears with obscenities. Gina has closed her eyes, her head bent far back, bravely enduring everything, though in the glow of the interior light I can see exactly that she is shivering slightly as waves of pleasure surge through her body.

I have lost track of time. The men are getting louder and louder, taking turns groping Gina's body and becoming ever more demanding, their lustful noises ever more ecstatic. I, too, am getting more and more aroused by the show and have long started fondling myself, slowly but surely catapulting myself towards a climax.

Suddenly, Gina opens her eyes while a stranger is

licking her breasts. Our eyes meet, our glances merge; everything around us becomes blurred, unimportant, and together we plunge into a first mind-blowing orgasm that shouldn't be the last that night ...

Creative Sexuality

Carmen from K. (37): I would like to tell you how I was introduced to the world of creative sex. It was a former colleague of mine who showed me the way, and today I'm very, very grateful he did (today he's my husband!).

I had started to flirt heavily with him, and we had gone on a few dates to get to know each other better. He knew I was divorced and that I had been without a partner for some time. Therefore I had to be sexually starved!

Little by little he confessed to me that he liked *something special* in bed. Although I blushed when he said that, he must have seen in my face that I was pleasantly aroused. He asked me quite directly if I had ever thought of something like that. I was totally perplexed and embarrassed — since he had hit a very sensitive nerve, because that was one of the reasons why my marriage had broken up: in bed, things had become absolutely boring between my former husband and me, and though I had numerous erotic fantasies I was extremely inhibited and somehow couldn't live them out. I just couldn't change my spots. But that was about to change now ...

When Frank, my colleague, now raised the subject of my sexual fantasies, I began to falter. He recognized my communication problems and said: *„It just annoys me that two people may think the same thing but can't manage to talk* about it! That's a paradox, isn't it? But I know something that could help us bring together our erotic desires ... "

Then he abruptly changed the subject and left me feeling uncertain.

But not for long, because the very next day — I had spent a restless night, time and again imagining what it would be like to sleep with Frank — a surprise was waiting for me when I came to the office. A thick, closed briefcase was lying on my chair with a folded note attached to it:

Something to browse through later, when you're alone at home ...

PS: Mark the places that really turn you on, put everything back in the briefcase and then put it on my desk! I'm looking forward to it!

Frank

I could hardly wait to grab the briefcase and retreat to the ladies' room to take a quick look at it. It just about took my breath away when I opened it, because inside I found a few special magazines that showed and explained some bizarre erotic varieties. Frank had covered all the bases: there was a small book on the subject of the *KamaSutra*, which is all about old East-Indian lovemaking techniques, a magazine on the subject of bizarre sex with pictures of people in rubber masks and latex suits, another dealing with various S/M practices, and last but not least he had included a relatively soft-core book featuring very beautiful, aesthetic photos of couples or threesomes during sex in various places with the title: *More fun during sex*. This book was accompanied by an explanatory factual text all around the subject of eroticism.

I didn't see Frank the whole day because he was away on business, which he had probably arranged on purpose. I could hardly wait to get home and take my time to look at the books and magazines. All comfy and wrapped in my bathrobe I lay down on my bed and began to leaf through it. After all, I had never seen anything like that before! A pity, actually, because I began to sense what I had missed.

I let the photos take an effect on me and marked those I liked especially with a yellow sticker. Little by little I felt how the photos turned me on, and I liked it. It was a completely new experience that I would never have made on my own!

When I was finished I had marked a total of eight pages: three positions from the KamaSutra that I found especially tempting (he loves her from behind, the »69« position and one where he kneels in front of her and pushes her legs high in the air during penetration); three pages from the softcore book with the suggestions for having more fun with sex (a couple is doing it outdoors in a meadow, another couple in the car and sex on the desk in the office); and two photos from the bizarre-sex magazine (he is wearing leather pants that are open in front and has his partner, wearing a latex bodice, tied up and laid out across a table while he is giving it to her from behind; and secondly — here I hesitated for the longest time! — a photo in which three erotic actors can be seen — a man and two women …)

That night I had really wild dreams, and when I woke up in the morning I vaguely remembered that I had come in my sleep.

I drove to the office extra early and put the briefcase back on Frank's desk as he had asked me to. I was excited like a school girl! When I finally met him briefly in the cafeteria during lunch hour, he smiled at me meaningfully. He didn't have much time, though, because he was looking after a supplier who was visiting, and he told me he would call me the next day.

It was Saturday, the weather was glorious and Frank picked me up for a little *jaunt* through the countryside. I had no idea what he had in mind when I got into his convertible, wearing a light summer dress. We were in good spirits as we set out for the countryside where Frank parked the car next to a secluded lake, and then he said:

"Carmen, you are a wonderful woman. You have no idea how much erotic potential is hiding inside of you, and your first husband must be a complete idiot for not having seen that!"

I blushed and lowered my head while he continued:

"Your hints have shown me that you are very sensual and sexually curious; it's just hard for you to show it. But that's what I'm here for now. I have fallen in love with you and I will open up an exciting world to you that you didn't even imagine existed! Leave it up to me, I will guide you ..."

Then he got out, went around the car, opened the door for me so I could get out and led me to the meadow where we made love for the first time, very tenderly and lovingly.

That was three years ago, and today I know: Frank is the man who fulfils all my hidden sexual desires. He knows exactly how to take me — in the true sense of the word!

He prepares everything necessary for our sometimes bizarre erotic sessions, as he did on that night when I was allowed to experience a threesome for the first time:

Frank wanted to take me out and had asked me to dress especially sexy; he would have a surprise for me. My appear—ance had also changed a lot in the three months we had been

officially together. My hairdo no longer looked — as it did
before — like that of a shy wallflower, but I had become more
self-assured. My newly won (or better given), freer sexuality
was also reflected in my clothing. That's why that night I
decided on a tight, black satin dress that brought out my good
figure. When Frank picked me up he whistled approvingly
through his teeth, and his admiring look told me that he was
pleased. But just before we left my flat he said:

„*Are you wearing anything underneath?*"

„*What?*", I asked confused.

„*If you're wearing anything under that dress, a slip, for
instance. If yes, then I would like you to take it off now.*"

Then he went out to the car to wait for me there.

After I had overcome my first confusion I reached
under my dress and slipped the black satin panties down over
my thighs. I carelessly left them behind in the hallway. Then I
plunged into my next adventure with Frank ...

We drove to a classy restaurant in which Frank had
reserved a table for us that was tucked away in a quiet corner.
After we had eaten a wonderful dinner during which we had
exchanged several promising looks and kisses, he moved right
next to me on the velvet-covered seat I was sitting on. From
our somewhat hidden *vantage point* the two of us were now
looking into the fairly crowded room that was doused in
romantic light. Suddenly I felt Frank's hand stray below across
my lap and between my thighs. When his fingers reached my
pubic area after a while, I was afraid I'd be dripping with lust
and leave spots on the expensive carpet under me, that's how
much I was aroused by this dangerous game!

And Frank didn't stop there. „*Just stay calm, my little
one, and let yourself go. I alone control your arousal!*" he

whispered in my ear, and I thought I would die with desire. He brought me to the edge of madness and I was shivering with pleasure. When I could hardly stand it anymore and was feverishly waiting for the relief of a climax, he suddenly stopped. He paid the bill while I was calming down again, then we left the restaurant.

The indecent caresses under the table had just been a way of getting me ready. What followed was an intoxicating night during which Frank and Svenja — our new playmate — took turns indulging me. First Frank had to tie me to the bed of the hotel room in which she was already waiting for us, wearing a breathtaking red evening dress, and cover my eyes with a mask so I could overcome my inhibitions. But then I abandoned myself completely to his wishes, which were:

„Let me see how you do it with a woman before my eyes, how you abandon yourself completely to your secret desires and rid yourself of your inhibitions with every scream of pleasure!"

And that I did all night. I fulfilled Frank's erotic wish to be a voyeur while I was hearing, tasting, feeling and smelling Svenja; and at the same time he made one of my most secret erotic fantasies come true — one of many still to follow …

The Crimson Letter: Fear and Lust

Tom from G. (36): Since this morning it had been sitting there in your letterbox: the crimson envelope that let you know it was time again. Our ritual had begun. But you still didn't know where it would lead you this time. A crimson envelope, it was always a blood-red envelope in which I told you my wishes which you had to follow. That's how I wanted it from you.

When you opened it you found a copied section of an old book describing a public lashing in detail. I knew this would instil fear in you; fear and lust …

I picked you up at three in the afternoon. Everything between us was the same as always — a completely normal couple going on a trip. We drove far out of town, through small villages and wonderfully green scenery. Sometime or another we turned into a country lane and finally stopped. I sensed you were insecure. That was good, because I knew that insecurity increases desire, arousal.

After a short hike we came to a small lake. Idyllic, out of the way. We changed into our swimsuits and jumped in the water. You hadn't bothered putting on your bikini top, and I could clearly see your nipples growing hard. What may have been the reason: the cold water or your burgeoning lust? No matter, it was my *cue* to start with today's disciplinary action at any rate.

„*What a fucking bitch you are!*" I flew in her face. „*Can't hold back your lust again! But I will enjoy teaching you some control …*"

When we were back at the shore and after we had dried ourselves off, I slowly went to our backpack and took out a rope, giving you a challenging look. Then we went a ways into the woods, while I was pulling you along by the arm.

"Please, Tom, I'm not sure we're really alone here. What if somebody comes along?" her question broke through the silence.

I just laughed and stopped because I had found a suitable tree. An old beech tree. Filtered by the crown, the sunlight fell in long rays onto the thick trunk. Yes, that was exactly the right place for the ritual I had planned for today.

You went up to the tree voluntarily and leaned against it — with your back to the trunk.

"No, Lena, while that's good of you, I want you to turn around and face the tree", I ordered you.

Suddenly your eyes went wide with alarm, because I guess you now remembered the copy of the text in the red envelope; the public lashing ...

You were breathing heavily when I turned you around and wrapped your arms around the trunk; now you were at my mercy — once again. But we had never done it this way, in public, in the great outdoors — with whip in hand!

I left you behind and went back to our place by the lake. There I sat down and enjoyed the feeling of power. You would be quite afraid now, with all kinds of thoughts crossing your mind. When would I come back? What would happen then? Would it hurt? What if some stranger saw you like that? Would I come back alone or bring somebody along? How long would it take? Would I even leave you there overnight? Would you be satisfied in the end, or would I leave you alone with your desire ...? So many questions and no answer — that's what made up the appeal of the ritual!

I stayed away for about an hour, then I took the whip

out of my backpack and went back. You were quietly waiting for my next move. I stood there, enjoying this unbelievably aesthetic view: you, almost naked, only wearing your bikini bottom, tied to the tree, your firm ass turned towards me, your arms stretched far around the trunk, your head lowered and buried between your shoulders. A glorious picture!

„You know what's in store for you and why you're being punished, don't you?"

Your answer came quietly and hesitantly: *„You will teach me some discipline, because I always get hot so fast and I can't control my lust."*

„And you really want this punishment and will enjoy it so that you can learn from it?" I kept on provoking her.

„Yes, I will try ..."

„Then you have to tell me after each lash what you're feeling!"

Just thinking of what sounds you would make and what it would look like when I would soon whip your behind turned me on! How much had I been looking forward to it, and now you would be obedient, willingly accept my gift of punishment and share your bizarre feelings with me!

I went up to you and brushed along your spine with the whip. Then I grabbed one of your butt cheeks with one hand and kneaded it. You gave a loud groan because this whole ritual turned you on. I could make out fine drops on your back — was it cold sweat, water from the lake that was dripping from your long hair you hadn't dried off yet, or was it because of the sticky heat of summer? Anyway, the wetness of your bikini bottom would intensify the lashes ...

I stepped back until I stood about two metres behind you and asked you:

„*Are you ready?*"

My hand was shaking with excitement when you replied:

„*Yes, I'm ready.*"

Whack, the first lash came down on your bottom. It made a wonderfully splashy, keen sound.

„*I'm listening!*" I reminded her.

„*It, it hurts!*"

Then the second and third lash came in quick succession, after which I paused again.

Your voice now sounded huskier, more aroused when you said:

„*It burns like fire on my ass — but not only there!*"

Number four and five followed, and I kept drilling you, wanted to hear from you:

„*Where else, where else do you feel it?*"

You fidgeted with your bottom and answered:

„*It's tingling like hell in the middle, between my legs!*"

Whack. I had placed number six especially well. It landed low on your right butt cheek, exactly where your bikini bottom ended and the naked flesh began. You winced and moaned.

I had an idea: I quickly stepped forward and pushed the cloth into your crack so that your entire butt was exposed now. That would sting nicely!

You threw your head far back in anticipation of the next lash.

„*Seven!*" I counted out loud, and you squeezed out between clenched teeth: „*Ahh, fuck it, my whole body is burning below!*"

Number eight, nine and ten left a red pattern on your

skin and made you go weak in the knees, because you were obviously close to have your first orgasmic convulsions. I knew you would love it! Now only a few more lashes until the ecstatic finale. I, too, could hardly hold back!

I took good aim and warned you to scream your feelings for me out loud because I wanted to know what it's like for you to be brought to an orgasm with lashes. When the whip came down the last four, five times you groaned lustfully and screamed ecstatically:

„*Yeah, that's what I need, I want your punishment, I want to learn discipline from your hand, it's so good, so fucking good – I'm coming …*"

Crying with happiness you were hanging in the ropes, couldn't stand up anymore, and I untied you and put you down on the mossy ground where I held you in my arms and stroked your head. You looked at me with veiled eyes and said:

„*I would never have dreamt it could be so wonderful! Thank you, Tom …*"

What would my next crimson letter hold in store for you? I didn't know yet, but there were still many exciting BD/SM games; I guess I would think of something …

Just a Single Scream ...

Lydia from A. (25): I guess I must have passed out for some time. I feel myself kind of waking up and for the first time see myself lying where I must have been lying for hours already. The cold that has long reached my naked feet, legs and even my bare bottom sits like an icy clamp on my unprotected, isolated private parts. I'm lying, hanging on the floor in front of your desk. I'm unable to move at all. I look around me and try to remember ...

Above me I see the two open leather straps from which I must have freed myself, because you didn't open them, that much I still remember. Without a second's hesitation you had turned around and were gone. After this scream, the first one: and which, as I knew now, many more were to follow when I realized you had really left me here all alone. I can't remember how much time has passed already. Will you come back and forgive me? Everything seems so unreal ...

I know you had warned me explicitly. *„If you make a single sound, if you scream, then it's all over"*, you had said. And I knew you really meant it. Then our ritual had started. You had led me to your study with the large, heavy oak desk at which your father and his father before him had already sat. Then you had told me to lie across it, and you had tied the leather straps around my wrists. I was strapped to the desk and was waiting for my lesson.

As always, it took awhile before you came back from the adjoining room where we kept our special utensils. I was already naked, and I didn't know if maybe you had undressed, too. But that was unlikely, because usually you remained fully dressed and initially treated me in a way other than the usual one between a man and a woman. That was part of the ritual.

Then I noticed that your pants were open. After all! Today I would finally be allowed to feel all of you again! But the question was, when. This knowledge made me crazy with anticipation ...

You stepped behind me without a word, and suddenly I felt something incredibly cold being pressed between my thighs. I was so surprised and the sensation was so strong that I instinctively reared up, sucking air through my teeth. I could hear a loud hissing sound. You pressed the can — for it had to be a can that came directly from the freezer — on my most sensitive, my most feminine parts. The sensation was incredible, and flashes of pleasure went through my brain.

You stepped back and I heard you say:

„*Remember your promise, love!*"

I closed my eyes and pressed my lips tight together, because I wanted to bravely bear your next onslaught, too — it would surely be more intense than the first one! Shortly afterwards I felt your hand directly on my button. With pleasurable, circular motions you massaged my lust centre, your fingers were gentle and warm. You are truly masterful when it comes to giving pleasure, because you know exactly how to drive a woman crazy. Single-mindedly you whipped up my desire, and my pelvis already began to jerk. Not long now, and I would ...

It hit me like a bolt of lightning! What was it? Oh God, the pain — a sensation I had never experienced before in this intensity went right through me. I heard you moan, and through a fog of pain and lust I felt your fingers continue to work me at the same time. Your motions became even stronger and more demanding, the pain was unbearable — unbearably sweet! — , and a giant orgasmic wave flooded me in a huge explosion. I tore at the leather straps, jerked and tossed around in my ecstatic delirium, and then I heard myself scream with pleasure ...

The last thing I registered through my foggy perception was how you slowly zipped up your pants and left the room without turning back once.

That's how it had happened; I hadn't stuck to the ritual, had broken my promise. Now I was sitting here, empty and abandoned. I noticed a small, silver clamp lying next to me on the floor. So that's what had triggered my momentous disobedience. This clamp had caused the incredible pain, for you had clamped it on my button ...

What now? A feeling takes hold of my body that can't be compared to anything else. I'm endlessly confused, forlorn, anxious, all I can do is wait for you and your punishment. All would be well if you'd only come back and punish me! All my thoughts are focused on that.

It's not until much later that I realize all this was part of your game. My fear is part of your punishment. You knew I would scream and that you would have to leave me behind — at least for awhile. Having me go through this time of immeasurable anxiety, despair and painful longing for you and your exciting lessons was the only way you could set up the special conditions and prepare me for our next ritual!

Today I know: in BD/SM games nothing happens without a purpose, there's a reason for every pain, every punishment, every seemingly senseless action. It is another building block in our house of absolute sexual fulfilment!

Pleasurable Torments through Unfairness and Tyranny

Ruth from E. (43): The steps were very steep and the light was diffuse. My husband led me on a leash down the narrow stairs to the cellar. When we got there, I had to kneel down and wait with lowered head. I couldn't make out much, but I sensed the presence of other people. Today the time had finally come: I was being taken out by my husband the way I had dreamt of for a long time!

The other guests gazed at me; I could feel it. He had first made it perfectly clear to me that I was to behave like a real slave — otherwise he would never discipline let alone take me here again! So the future of my absolute, boundless lust depended on how I would act today …

I had already passed the first test, because for a brief moment I could see admiration in his eyes when he picked me up for my *debut*. So he liked my outfit: a really tight, black latex corset, black net stockings, incredibly high-heeled shoes and perfect make-up, for which I had taken a lot of time. I had also pinned up my hair in an elaborate hairdo. So I had already taken the first hurdle, for my appearance seemed to be suitable for the occasion to which he would take me today.

Basically I already knew what a slave was supposed to do and not to do, that is how she had to behave. For privately, just between him and me, my husband had already shown me the meaning of obedience. But I hadn't stopped making small mistakes (e.g. not lowering my head when he talked to me), for which I was then being punished — in the most exciting way! But would I be able to keep up my role as slave in the presence of others? I suspected he would be unfair to me, would take pleasure in deliberately tyrannizing me before the eyes and ears of the others present. Would I pass the test? I didn't really know, and I was nervous. What if I made a mistake and ruined everything? Then I would never again be allowed to experience the pleasurable torment of his punishment ...

I had already blundered once, about three weeks before. In the morning he had announced that he wanted to find me *prepared* when he came home in the evening. I already knew what that meant: to be stretched out across the sofa with my butt sticking out provocatively, blindfolded and waiting for deliverance from my tormenting lust. I had felt this indefinable buzz of arousal in my body all day long and had feverishly waited for the evening, anxious and horny at the same time. By the early afternoon I couldn't concentrate any longer and therefore decided to find some distraction. I wanted to quickly zip into town to get him a special present: I wanted to wear long, black leather boots — nothing else — when he would find me ready in the evening!

No sooner said than done. I took the train into town (we live a ways outside) and from there the bus to the centre. That day I hardly took notice of my surroundings. Instead, I kept seeing highly erotic images in my mind's eye and even thought I could already feel him on and in my body!

After some time I had finally found a store that was carrying erotic fashion and accessories. I took particular care choosing the high-shafted boots — I knew he would have liked that, too. He liked it if you also paid attention to the small details of the game, and I was proud of myself, because in seeing this through his eyes instead of mine I had begun to behave like a real slave. That was real humility!

But far from it. Because in my excitement about choosing the new boots I had completely lost track of time. I had just missed the train I had wanted to take in order to be back in time to prepare myself for the evening. There was nothing I could do but wait for the next one — which didn't leave for an hour yet!

I became anxious but tried to calm myself with the thought I might still be able to make it. Normally he wouldn't be home before 6 p.m., and if I ran from the station I might get home just in time. When I finally pushed open the front door, completely out of breath, and saw his heavy, black coat hanging in the wardrobe, it already dawned on me. My heart skipped a beat and my throat constricted. Now it was obvious: I had failed as a slave.

My husband was sitting in the living room, a fire crackling in the fireplace. In his left hand he was holding a glass of red wine, in his right a cigar. He looked me over with stony eyes, and I lowered my head.

„I don't want to hear your excuses. You've disappointed me, and there's no excuse for that", he said in a calm, matter-of-fact tone. Then he noticed the bag with the boots in my hand. I took them out without a word and held them out for him. Perhaps he would be more lenient?

„And remember one thing: I am the one who is dressing you. You're not allowed to decide what to wear as a slave!"

Then he stood up and left the house without a word. Since then — as I said, this happened about three weeks ago — he has been extremely cool to me. I put on a brave face and endured this punishment, because I hoped it would be over sometime, which turned out to be the case. Three days ago he finally told me he would give me a real chance to prove myself as a slave. He would take me to a party at which I would have to play my role perfectly. Now it was up to me to make the best of it ...

I had been feverishly waiting for this day and was hardly able to sleep last night with excitement. I was carried away by my sexual imagination running wild in my head, and for me these fantasies are a big part of the appeal. I see the time between the announcement of an erotic adventure or a punishment until its final implementation as one of the most pleasurable and exciting times altogether!

Finally, the time had come: he picked me up and we drove to the mansion where my public premiere as a slave was supposed to take place. When we had arrived at the bottom of the stairs and I was kneeling with lowered head on the cold stone floor, I was overcome by an incredible calmness after awhile. I felt my senses were suddenly hypersensitive to everything happening around me. I listened to my husband, who was quietly talking to someone. He still held me tight on the leash, and I became aroused as people let their eyes roam over my body. Unfortunately, I could only make out fragments of what my husband was saying. *„First time ... as a test ... hang in there ... learn some discipline...“*, I heard from my husband, while *„hot chassis ... tight ass ... nice, big tits ... borrow ...“* were the words I could make out from whoever he was talking to. I flinched: would my husband leave me to the desires of others today? I wasn't prepared for that! Still, I could feel the unmistakable signs of my arousal growing at the thought of it!

Quite some time must have passed already. He had led me on the leash around the room while he was talking to the others and drinking champagne. I was thirsty, too, he had to know that, but instead of giving me something to drink he let a few drops of the precious, ice-cold liquid drip on my back and butt from time to time — to the laughter and cheers of those present. The cold champagne trickled over my body into my corset and between my butt cheeks. I heard the tinkle of glasses and the babble of voices, and slowly my knees and back began to hurt. But until now I had meekly endured everything.

Suddenly he bent down to me, gently stroked my back and announced for everyone to hear:

„Well, my little one, I'm ready. Now I really want to present you as my willing slave for the first time — and don't you dare make a single sound, because then it's all over right away! I'm going to take what I want from you now."

He knew exactly that these words turned me on no end, and now he took the fine, black silk scarf he was wearing around his neck to blindfold me. Then he took me up in his arms and carried me to a kind of stone pedestal — that's what it felt like — in the middle of the room. All around me I could hear the voices of the other guests cheering us on with obscenities and getting wilder by the minute. Now and then I could feel a third hand or a brief flick of a stranger's tongue on me while I was writhing under the lustful caresses of my husband.

He didn't have to take his time getting me ready — the last days of uncertain anticipation of the upcoming sexual adventure had been all the preparation I needed for my sensuality! I just loved letting myself be led by him and submitting to his will. The blindfold was very helpful here because it allowed me to feel anonymous, though I knew exactly that all the others could see me. It also allowed me to resist the temptation to open my eyes and possibly break the spell I was under. I was entirely immersed in my dark world of lust, without light and without uttering a single sound. That was an additional torment for me, because the things he was doing to me carried me away in huge waves of arousal, and I had a hard time not to moan or whimper. His lustful treatment made me twitch in ecstasy; I was trembling under his powerful, demanding motions that got me so excited. His stamina was tormenting me, and yet I was longing for more!

When my husband finally turned me around to put me in a different position for the umpteenth time, putting me on all fours, and I could feel the hard stone under my knees, his sexual power and strange hands on my breasts at the same time, I finally lost all control: in the throes of a sheer endless climax I passed out …

I didn't wake up and open my eyes until much later, on our way home.

„Did I scream?" was my first anxious question, and my husband answered with a gentle smile:

„No, darling, you were the most wonderful, submissive slave I could have wished for!"

The Punishment Notice

Svea from G. (31): Shortly before I went to this interview it had arrived, the notice that I would be punished tonight. Jochen knew I would give you this interview; he had given me permission to tell you about our disciplining games — anonymously, of course! He surely wouldn't take back the punishment notice now — and I've got about 12 hours (counting from this morning) to get ready for it in my mind! This time of preparation is a significant part of the punishment itself, which consists of four acts: notice, preparation, execution, reconciliation. If you're not familiar with this chronological breakdown, you can hardly understand how effective it is, because one is forced to deal with the ever approaching punishment. And that's how it is today, too. None of my colleagues in the office has any idea that I would get a good hiding with the riding crop tonight! Only you are in the know, now, and I will tell you how things will probably proceed. I will describe to you how I see tonight unfold in my mind's eye — and I find that enormously exciting!

I openly admit: I'm really scared of each punishment; but I also know that it's beautiful beyond comparison to be loved by Jonathan afterwards, and these two feelings contradict each other. Right now I'm still afraid, afraid of the riding crop — oh, it stings like hell ...!

How I imagine tonight? Well, it'll go something like this:

Once at home, I will still have a little time to get dressed, and the second act, the preparation, can begin. I don a tight bodice that especially highlights my hips and breasts and fumble to attach the stockings to the garter belt. Next come my discipline panties made of black, shiny taffeta satin with high-cut leg openings. They fit snugly around my butt without a wrinkle, and tight elastics around the openings guarantee a tight fit. High-heeled shoes round off my outfit, and I take a look at myself in the full-length dressing mirror.

Nice, very nice, but I'm not done yet. I still have to fetch the whip, which I fearfully let slide through my fingers, and put out the straps to be tied with — because I would never be able to stand the announced 25 lashes without a struggle! These preparations, which I have to do myself, are very arousing and only increase my inner restlessness and fear ...

I hear Jonathan come home and my erotic fear — maybe that's a possible definition — reaches a peak. What will he do next? Or will he let me stew awhile, all done up in my discipline outfit? He takes me in his arms, kisses me, and I am trembling with lust when his hands cup my panty-clad butt. These hands can be infinitely tender: I can feel them. But they can also be strict and resolute: I love them. I abandon myself to these caresses. How wonderful it is to be touched and felt up this way. The lust in me comes alive and I whisper in Jonathan's ears:

„Darling, please do it!"

Stretched across and tied to the spanking bench I see myself in the three-piece dressing mirror. Jonathan is holding the whip in his hand, tenderly tracing my full curves with it while I am anxiously waiting for the first burning lash. Between my legs, everything is tingling with pleasure. And then it comes down on me, biting into my tender flesh. I'm arching my back on the bench — uhhh, how it stings! I ride out this lash, the next one and the one after that, but then I'm getting loud and Jonathan grants me a short break ...

On it goes, and sometime later I hear him announce

the last five and order me to stick out my butt even more, and gasping and screaming I present my cheeks to him. The lashes go through and through me, but pleasure is also playing a role. Only four, only three, only two, only one left — then it's all over.

I have received my punishment, and now I find myself in Jonathan's arms. How wonderful it is to abandon myself so openly and wantonly to his skilful game. It's good to have a husband who understands me, who knows that he must punish me so he can bring me heaven on earth afterwards. When he unties me he can see how ready I am for him ...

Disciplining her in Public

Melanie from T. (24): I can't remember how everything started. I can only explain it like this: At some time or another our *normal* little games in bed hadn't been enough anymore; we had explored ever more extreme areas of sexuality, and over time Frederik had become ever stronger and me ever weaker with each time. It had absolutely nothing to do with brutality, because in the final analysis I did everything of my own free will. But it was always his desires we were living out together — though at the same time they were mine, it's just that I didn't dare fessing up to it all too openly, unlike him. That was his part, and he played it masterfully! And that was what made him seem so powerful to me.

I remember our first time in public very well. We had visited a museum together to see an art exhibition, and if you had no idea of our foible for BD/SM you would have thought we were two completely normal lovers. Hand in hand we were strolling through the rooms, commenting on the paintings when suddenly — from one second to the next — I could sense a change in Frederik. He let go of my hand and turned towards me, his voice becoming more determined and his eyes a shade darker. Then he said:

„It's time again, darling. The whole atmosphere here really turns me on. I want to feel you here and now!"

I was shocked and aroused at the same time! Here, out in public?! What if someone came along? No, I couldn't do that, that was against all morals I had been brought up with ...

And apparently it's exactly that which makes it so appealing to me. It's hard to understand for someone who's never felt that way. But it's really true: the game only turns me on so much because Frederik *forces* me; the experience in the museum excites me because it is something I would never have suggested myself because I simply can't change my spots. With his authority, Frederik helped me to let myself go. I surrendered any responsibility for what I was doing by submitting to his erotic will.

Half-heartedly I tried again to prevent the terrible, the delightful from happening, though I knew exactly that Frederik would insist even more — it's part of our game, as it were. I looked at him with wide open eyes and whispered:

„Frederik, please. I'm afraid. Think it over again. I don't want that ... "

But I knew the decision had long been made. There was no way back.

He grinned at me, pushed me in the nearest corner and answered:

„I know you want it, too. I'm sure of it. You dream of doing it in public, just like me. And because you don't have

the courage to tell me you will now suffer the consequences, my little yellow 'delinquent'!"

Then he slowly put one hand under my summer coat. Since I was only wearing a thin dress underneath, I could immediately feel his warm hand through the fabric honing on my burning privates. I could feel how much the situation turned me on, for my breasts reacted, too, pushing the signs of my arousal through the fabric. Within seconds my misgivings were gone and replaced by a breathless desire; within seconds his sure touch between my thighs and skilful massage of my most sensitive spot had broken all my willpower, so that I was trembling with pleasure.

Quick as a flash, Frederik suddenly withdrew, cynically laughing out loud and walking back a few steps. While I was looking around the room with a start to see if someone was coming, he didn't even turn his head, that's how sure he was of his power, his authority. Instead, he crossed his arms and said:

"Pull up your dress and look at me. Don't you dare close your eyes!"

I reacted like in a trance.

"Yeah, that's it, that's how I like it. Now spread your legs and push your panties to the side a little so I can see better. Now stroke it with your finger and feel the wetness. Tell me what you feel."

My voice was thin and cracked, and my legs were about to give out. Tears were welling up in my eyes — but not for pain. It was a combination of a kind of stimulating shame because of the humiliation and boundless arousal resulting from it!

"It's warm ...", I whispered and wanted to close my

eyes so I wouldn't have to look directly at any stranger who happened to come in.

Frederik's voice, however, remained calm:

"Again, louder, I can't hear you. And keep looking at me. I want to see the lust in your eyes!"

Millimetre by millimetre I pushed my finger inside, only to pull it back again the next moment. It felt like it wasn't me who was acting, but as if Frederik was controlling me with his gaze. With relish he would squat down now and then, taking deep breaths so he would be able to smell and savour the steamy musk of my lust, and then would stand up again in front of me with crossed arms.

Automatically, my motions became faster, I sucked in the dominant look in his eyes and got swept away in rapturous sensuality. There was a certain point beyond which I couldn't hold back any longer. I submitted to his will, did what he demanded, was his marionette. My finger became faster and faster, ever more urgent, until I suddenly threw back my head and screamed in ecstasy. While I was sliding down against the wall I felt Frederik's arms pick me up and his lips close my mouth ...

A moment later we were already walking arm in arm towards the exit. A museum employee was running towards us and asked what had happened. He had heard something like a scream.

"Oh, it's nothing. My girl friend just had a little dizzy spell, but now she's ok again. She just needs a little fresh air", Frederik explained to him, and as we were walking out the door he held my musky finger under his nose with a mischievous grin full of pleasure ...

Back home, we pounced on each other like animals.

My Greatest Wish: Anal Sex

Peter from K. (43): I have wanted to try out anal sex for a long time. The thought of *sex through the backdoor* really turned me on and I've been haunted by fantasies of it since I first heard about it. I had bought myself special magazines revolving around the subject. I had devoured every report dealing with it, and that had stimulated my erotic fantasy enormously. Up to now there had never been the right *opportunity* to experience anal sex for real. My former partners had been strictly against it, and I also hadn't been able to convince them to try it out once.

Gradually it became clear to me, though, that I shouldn't wait for my current girl friend Brenda to confess this wish to me on her own — then I would probably never get to enjoy this erotic experience! Instead, I had to make sure she would share that wish with me. I had to get her excited about the thought of trying out anal sex, then she would actually give herself over to this special pleasure sometime! So I somehow had to devise a situation that would automatically lead to Brenda offering herself to me in this way, that would leave her NO CHOICE! But how? I thought about it for a long time.

One winter evening — outside, snowflakes were falling softly while we were curled up in front of the fireplace with a glass of mulled wine — the time had finally come. We both were in a very affectionate mood, and when over time I sensed that Brenda was being especially amorous that night, I decided to indulge her in a very special way — that is the *Greek* way! However, I didn't want to force her under any circumstances. One thing was clear for me: she should be so hot for it that she would be the one asking me to make love to her anally!

First I blindfolded her with a cloth, which reinforced the impression of a helpless victim for both of us. I just loved it to see her so helpless, and she loved to surrender to this helplessness. I stroked and caressed her forever and turned her around every now and then so I could kiss and massage her from the other side. Brenda was practically melting under my hands, and sometime later I pulled out a rope I had got and laid out earlier. Brenda already knew this little game. It was nothing new to her that I was the dominant one and she the submissive one in bed. Every now and then she loved indulging in our special bondage games, loved being tied up and *used* by me as I saw fit; that always turned us on enormously.

Brenda was lying on her belly and had her eyes closed when I slowly pulled up her arms and tied the soft rope around her wrists. She sighed and smiled and now had her hands stretched far above her head; I eventually tied her to the leg of an armchair so that she couldn't turn on her back anymore.

I grabbed a bottle of massage oil and dripped a few drops on her back. Slowly and deliberately I rubbed the liquid into her soft, tanned skin and casually said:

„*Today I've got something very special in mind for you, something you will never forget …*"

At the same time I would let my massaging fingers slip between her butt cheeks again and again, spreading the oil there. Brenda was already moaning, and I noticed that she spread her legs a little all on her own. So she wanted to encourage me to go there and was longing for my tender caresses in the centre of her lust. But I was going to make her wait for that for a long time yet! Until she was whimpering with desire!

I kneaded her butt cheeks with both hands and she downright pushed her hips towards me. Eventually she pulled herself up a little so that now she was kneeling on all fours, her hands still tied to the bottom of the armchair. This position allowed me to catch an extremely suggestive sight of her, seeing as she was wonderfully ready for lovemaking! But it wasn't quite time yet ...

I knelt directly behind her and reached around her body so that I could stimulate her breasts which were hanging down in this position. She was enormously sensitised, because as soon as I touched her small, erect pearls and firmly took them between my thumb and forefinger, she winced with pleasure. She sighed and moaned when I took a firmer grip with both hands and started to work on her breasts more expectantly. I lightly pulled on her nipples, and Brenda reacted by moaning loudly and insistently pushing her butt towards me. Her whole body was covered with tiny droplets of sweat. I had never seen her so hot! At the same time I asked her provocatively:

„Well, my little mare, do you like that or should I work you a little harder?"

All the while I kept on checking the heat between her thighs with one hand and alternately stimulating her breasts with the other.

No question: Brenda was more than ready! But the decisive part of my preparations was still missing. I pulled out a special anal stimulator from a cardboard box I had set out beforehand. First I slowly stroked along her spine down to her crack and up again with the softly humming vibrator. Brenda shuddered, seeing that she could only feel something vibrating but not see exactly what it was. She was still tied to the armchair and kneeling on all fours. She still had no idea what this toy was aimed at. But she was no longer able to think clearly anyway. Instead she was shivering with pleasure and arousal and kept pushing her most intimate regions towards me without any shame or reservations.

„*Do you still need a little oil between your legs, or is that enough?*" I asked her, though I could see the oily wetness already running down her thighs. I asked her to tell me if she could imagine being conquered with a vibrator. „*Tell me what you think that would feel like, or I'll stop at once and leave you here all tied up!*" I ordered her.

„*It will massage me inside — everywhere! The thing will conquer me with your help, and you will nearly drive me crazy with it!*" Brenda told me with shaky voice and panting with lust at her exciting visions. While she was telling me that, I let my outstretched middle finger shoot out from time to time, to which she reacted with loud, disjointed sighs ...

„*Yeah, but that's not all. Can you imagine this thing is only supposed to prepare you for something very special?!*" I asked her, and Britta's body tensed up for a second. The next moment a shiver of excitement ran through her skin and she began to whimper and push up against me even more. The image of what I was about to do with her must have set off a fireworks of lust in her head which immediately spread to her genitals. She was practically washed away with desire and her fears and reservations were entirely displaced by her uncompromising wish to be finally satisfied. Later on she told me that more than anything it was the thought of doing it the *Greek* way which drove her to a state of sexual frenzy. She was tied up, extremely aroused, kneeling in a submissive position like a bitch and was practically helpless — and was about to experience hot anal sex for the first time in her life!

She simply couldn't stand it anymore; I had *tormented* her for too long, had caused hot waves of pleasure to surge through her body only to stop shortly before she reached her climax. That was too much for her. With a despairing scream she called out:

„*Come on, take me, damn it. I want to feel you there, feel you deep inside of me ...*" as she invitingly pushed out her butt towards me.

That was exactly what I had been waiting for! Before I fulfilled this erotic wish for both of us I asked her again:

„*So, you really want it THAT way?*"

Then I felt her warm body engulf me and suck me up little by little ...

Waking the »Sleeping Dragon«

René from A. (37): I had long known that I still had to discover a lot about my sexuality. In retrospect — and on a subconscious level — it must have been clear to me for quite some time that as I was developing, so was my sexuality. Yes, I was happy with Anna. We had an entirely *normal* relationship, and sleeping with her was fun, too. But I knew there had to be more. Something inside of me was waiting to be set free. I just didn't know exactly what; but I probably always suspected it, because I happen to be more of the dominant type. One day I finally managed to wake the *sleeping dragon* in me, that is to finally live out my penchant for sexual dominance with Anna. At the same time it was most important for me not to scare her off, let alone hurt her, no matter what! A mishap should come to our aid here:

We had invited a few friends and Anna was preparing a tasty dinner. She was in a good mood, mucking around in the kitchen and setting the table, and while we were waiting for our guests we fooled around and drank a glass of red wine. She was wearing a tight-fitting dress showing the outlines of her body underneath, and I just couldn't help drawing her towards me and slipping my hands under her dress. We were smooching like that for a while when suddenly she jumped up as if something had bitten her and ran full of panic into the kitchen, from where the smell of something burning drifted towards me, confirming my suspicions: the lasagne had turned into a dark encrusted mess ...

Anna came out of the kitchen with tears in her eyes and told me what had happened. The dinner was ruined, and our guests would show up any minute. I wanted to cheer her up and ease the situation a little, and that's why I threatened her for fun with a cryptic smile on my face:

„*For that you'll get a severe punishment later!*" Then I turned around just like that and called the pizza service to order our dinner.

Anna was embarrassed about the ruined lasagne in front of our guests, and throughout the entire evening she would look at me sheepishly now and then — even though the evening turned out casual and relaxed, the food was delicious and we had a lot of fun. The red wine flowed generously, and in her frustration Anna drank more than usual. When in the course of the evening we met in the kitchen again I suddenly felt like continuing my punishment game, and without really thinking about it I told her with a twinkle in my eye:

„Well, my little wretch, are you already looking for-ward to your punishment for the ruined lasagne?"

She answered half playfully, but also with a certain gravity in her voice:

„Please forgive me! I promise it'll never happen again. What are you going to do with me?"

„You can be quite sure you will have to pay for it ...!" I fuelled her fear and left her standing in the kitchen.

The whole thing hadn't been planned but developed out of the situation. I'm sure the alcohol also contributed something because I was in fact more serious than I let on: I felt that these threats really turned me on, and while I went on talking to our guests, the thought of the upcoming punish-ment kept creeping into my mind. My fantasy was just about running wild, and I saw Anna, naked and tied to the bed, writhing under sweet torments ...

Anna was very quiet for the rest of the evening, but now and then our eyes would meet. Today I know that these were the first moments of our new and changed relationship, because it was a completely new dimension of living together in which we were moving that evening — and every day since. We looked at each other and I couldn't believe what I read in her eyes: fear and arousal!

Blood shot down to my lower parts, but it wasn't only there I felt my desire. BD/SM games take place above all in your head, stimulating the imagination. Now there was no turning back any more because Anna had signalled to me that she, too, had to go along with this game.

When our guests had left, she began to clear away the glasses. I didn't help her but stood behind her, arms crossed, and waited until she turned around to me. Then I said:

"Maybe you think you could get away without your punishment by cleaning up here. But I haven't forgotten. Leave everything and go up to the bedroom. There you will get undressed, lie on the bed and wait until I come!"

That was the moment of truth. Would Anna give herself over to this game as I thought I had seen in her eyes? Would she give our relationship a completely new dimension for the future, or would she lack the courage, after all?

Without a word she put the tray back on the table and went upstairs with lowered head ...

When I entered the bedroom a quarter of an hour later — I had made her wait that long on purpose because the uncertainty about what was in store for her was part of the game — Anna was lying naked on the bed. She was only wearing a black G-string and was stretched out on her back.

"I told you to be naked!" I admonished her in an authoritative voice and added: *"I might as well just add that to your punishment."* I grabbed her wrists and made her fingers grasp the bars of our bed. She had to leave them there until I allowed her to let go. Then I took off her G-string by just tearing it apart.

Now I started to lay out the various utensils I had brought up from downstairs beside the bed: a bowl with ice cubes, a leather belt, two silk ribbons, a special sex video (hardcore!) I had secretly bought, and a blindfold. I explained to her that I would only use the silk ribbons to tie her up if she didn't leave her arms in place on her own. The blindfold, too, would only be necessary in certain situations, depending on how she behaved. That made her even more insecure and her eyes had an anxious and vulnerable, but also an aroused and expectant look.

I took one of the ice cubes, put it in my mouth and bent down over her breasts. Startled, Anna sucked in her breath when I took one of her nipples between my lips and held the ice cube on it. In an instant she tensed up, arched her back, threw her head far back and closed her eyes. I would alternate *icing up* first one, then the other dark pearl, and I sensed that she liked this sweet torment.

„*That won't be all you'll have to endure today, not by a long shot!*" I threatened her. „*Tell me what the punishment is for!*"

And Anna complied: „*You, you're doing it because I ruined the dinner.*"

„*Right, what else?*"

„*I behaved badly, and that's why I must be punished*", she continued while I was massaging her breasts and circling her areolas with the ice cube between my fingers. As I told her to go on talking, I let the wet, cold pleasure tool slide downwards over her belly.

Now she was getting wilder by the minute, ever better in her servile comments. Hearing herself talk like that obviously turned her on — and me, too!

„*I will be patient and endure your punishment because I want to try and do better in future. You can do with me whatever you think is right — I'll hold still and accept your punishment!*"

Now I was reaching her genitals with the ice cube. Quickly and harshly I suddenly ran over them with the cold *instrument of torture*, and Anna flinched back as if struck by lightning, instinctively letting go of the bars.

„*You don't listen, do you? I guess I have to tie you up!*" I let her know and took the silk ribbons. When she was tied up I got undressed, my meanwhile fully erect member presenting itself to her. I got up from the bed and sat down comfortably in a chair that stood diagonally opposite to the bed against the wall. Then I put the video in the video recorder there, turned on the TV and wheeled the table into a position where both Anna and I could see the screen. Anna stared at me with baited breath. After all, I knew what we were about to see, and I was already looking forward to her reaction and my continued verbal and optical *tortures.*

While a dominator appeared on the screen who was wearing a bizarre black leather outfit and was servicing three bound women from behind who were kneeling in front of him on a table, I slowly reached down to pleasurably indulge myself. All kinds of moaning, whimpering and smacking noises from the video pervaded our bedroom, steeped in a diffuse light, and Anna alternately stared from the screen to my hand that was working with relish on my member. In between she would impatiently tear at the ribbons.

I let myself get really hot watching the video, savouring the highly erotic action on screen and at the same time the scurrilous situation between Anna and me. I could see how insecure she was: the video had added to her confusion. Was that what I was going to do with her today? How far would I go? Would I treat her the same way the man on the screen was treating his playmates one day?

After some time — the video kept playing in the background — I went over to the bed again and stood in front of her. Lustfully she stared at my menacing manhood and tried to reach it with her lips. I slipped my hands between her legs and began to massage her there, so that she was soon quivering and moaning impatiently. Over and over again she would glance at the TV where in the meantime one of the three women was servicing two men at the same time — a very juicy image that left nothing to the imagination ...

„*Who knows, maybe one day I'll do that with you if you don't listen!*" I let Anna know while my hands kept on working on her most sensitive area. She reacted with loud moaning. And when we finally joined our bodies after I had *tormented* her for a long time with unsettling words and harsh, quick touches, we both had an orgasm that eclipsed everything we had experienced before.

We both knew that this was a new beginning in our relationship, because we had pushed open a door that led us to a completely new realm of sensuality — a realm we probably had always secretly been longing for, but which we hadn't dared to enter.

Since then we are also practicing little punishment rituals in our everyday life together. For example, sometimes my little wretch has to wear a so-called vibro-slip (that I had bought in a specialty sex shop) under her normal clothing if she hadn't been listening again or if she had forgotten something. That thing keeps her in a state of erotic turmoil all day long with its intimate buzz, while I meticulously check whether Anna has followed my instructions. And I can see again and again that she, too, takes great pleasure in our game; much more than *normal* sex could ever have given her!

A »Decent« Woman ...

Daniela from W. (36): We were sitting quite a ways back in the dark theatre. I hadn't actually wanted to see the film at all, but as always Sven had talked me into it, and I had come along because he wanted me to. I was sitting in the chair, bored and hardly following the action anymore; it was a spy thriller, by the way. But suddenly I was totally spellbound by a bizarre scene: in an underground dungeon a female agent was being tortured by a man. She was naked and had her arms stretched far above her head, because her wrists were shackled in iron rings which in turn were fastened to the ceiling via a rope and pulley. The torturer had the other end of the rope in his hands. He was just telling her with a lecherous undertone in his voice and a sneer on his face what he intended to do with her ...

I felt how my hands became moist all of a sudden and my eyes were riveted to the screen. I had never seen anything like it! I was breathing harder because this scene turned me on no end — though I was also somehow embarrassed because of my reaction!

Sven gave me a sidelong glance, smiled and took my sweaty hand in his. He leaned over to me and whispered:

„You like that, darling?! He's going to punish his prisoner, and there's nothing she can do — she's helpless!"

I shuddered and my breaths came in fits and starts because now it began to dawn on me why Sven had dragged me into the cinema. He must have known ...

He took his time before he finally put an end to my impatient waiting. For more than two weeks I couldn't get the scene from the film out of my head. By nature I'm actually a rather quiet, low-key type of woman and it's never been easy for me to freely voice my sexual wishes. But Sven managed to uncover these wishes, though I never specifically mentioned them. And that's how it had happened this time, too: He had noticed my reaction in the cinema and knew I would basically be open to that kind of treatment. And that's how I knew he would also tie me up like that some day. I was getting more impatient from day to day. It was a combination of fear and excitement ...

Finally the time had come: He pulled me on the bed beside him, lovingly ran his fingers through my hair and felt how I began to relax. Sven gently kissed and caressed me, his tongue exploring my lips and my neck. Then he wrapped my long hair around one hand and gently pulled on it. My head automatically went backwards.

He slipped one hand under my blouse and pushed it up. My head was still bent back and he was holding me by the hair. I felt my breath come in fits and starts and kept my eyes shut. Sven didn't bother unbuttoning my blouse but tore it open in one go, buttons flying everywhere in the room. He carelessly tossed the ruined blouse aside and with a quick movement opened my bra which also landed somewhere beside the bed.

Sven must have planned this evening carefully and I could feel that he was enormously turned on in anticipation of things to come. When he went over my breasts with both hands I noticed by his firm grip that he, too, was in the grips of lust. He went over my skin with the tip of his tongue down to my belly button and opened my pants with agitated fingers. I pulled myself further up on the bed so that now I was lying there fully stretched out.

Suddenly Sven pulled my arms above my hand and

crossed my wrists. Now there was no longer any doubt: he wanted to tie me up! He reached to the side and produced a black, thin scarf out of the drawer of the bedside table, which he then tied around my wrists and to the bars at the head of our bed.

A shudder of arousal went through me in reaction to this. My nipples were hard and erect and my eyes transfigured with lust. Yet a trace of shame was still left in my thoughts and I doubted I could do something so indecent. I looked at him questioningly and opened my mouth to say something.

„Not a word", said Sven. „We do it my way!"

„Please don't hurt me!" was all I still managed to get out.

„No, darling, I won't hurt you — as long as you play along ...", he replied with a laugh.

Sven now got up and pulled off my pants, socks and panties with a single jerk. Now I was naked. Then he took two more scarves he had laid out beside the bed and wound them around my ankles. He spread my legs and tied each ankle to a bedpost. Now I was completely at his mercy.

He bent down to me and took a nipple between his teeth, working on it thoroughly. My hips began to twitch restlessly and I started to writhe under his eager caresses. The whole situation turned me on no end.

Suddenly Sven let off, stood up beside the bed and opened his pants with a smile. His arousal was highly visible.

„Please don't. I really can't do it. I'm a decent woman, after all ...", I whimpered softly.

He let his fingers slide over my genitals and answered:

„I don't think you are — otherwise you wouldn't be so prepared for me!"

With these words he drew close to my head. He bent over me and stroked my hair. Then he let his thumb wander over my face down to my lips, gently forced me to open my mouth and let me suck on his finger. When he pulled out his thumb after a while I had no choice but to grant him his wish. He knelt over me, supporting my head with both hands ...

This scene was a complete turn-on for both of us. For me, because I was practically forced to do things I had never done before and which were absolutely irreconcilable with my strict moral upbringing, and for Sven because he dominated me and my will. He taught me how to be his sexual servant — and at the same time satisfy my own indecent wishes!

Multiple Orgasms through Sexual Submission

Ella and Hans from H. (42 and 46):

Ella: Looking back at it I can't tell anymore what brought on my enthusiasm for BD/SM in our relationship. I just know that Hans skilfully and intentionally managed to bring out this proclivity in me at some point in time. This kind of erotic life together has given our partnership a very special impulse which I don't want to miss anymore. We've been practicing this kind of sex for about 10 years now — and it never gets boring! Maybe it's precisely that which makes BD/SM so appealing: it's never the same, but always has something new to offer. The range of experiences is endless. You can, better must, use your imagination, and then the game will never be dull or uninteresting.

I will try to explain to you why we settled on this special form of sensuality (actually, it was Hans, I only reacted to his actions). There were several factors coming together: First, about 10 years ago we had reached a point in our relationship where both of us realized it had simply *grown stale*. The initial infatuation including butterflies and hearts aflutter was over, but something else had taken its place: trust! In bed, however, we both had become a little more sedate, everything was a little more moderate — not to say boring! Even though both of us were sure that we still loved each other.

At the same time, that is to say parallel to this *external* development in our relationship, there was something going on inside each of us independent of each other. We were both thinking about ourselves ever more often, were analysing — whether consciously or subconsciously — our erotic fantasies and dreams, were asking ourselves what we had experienced until then and what we would still wish for. We were at an age (low/mid-30's) where the wild phase of sexuality is behind you and you either manage to set out for new and undiscovered shores or you stick to the familiar (many stay in their marriage/relationship without changing anything there and would rather have an affair).

Of course, all of that was going on in our heads without anyone noticing anything — not even the partner. It wasn't until much later that we realized we had been thinking about these things at the same time — and fortunately we set out on the same path!

That may sound like from one day to the next we had suddenly decided for ourselves to change our sexual inclinations or to finally live out our existing but hidden desires. But that's nonsense, of course. The whole thing was a long process that developed quite gradually. Step by step we had to check out what exactly our desires were and how far we would want to go with them. But Hans was the more determined one in this, because I am the more self-conscious, reserved type who doesn't like taking the initiative. My husband was the one who set off everything ...

Hans: Yes, because I wanted to save our relationship. I had the strong feeling that we were drifting apart and that we would become more and more unhappy and bored with each other if nothing was done. I knew I had certain sexual fantasies which I had never disclosed to Ella until then — for whatever reasons. Maybe I was still too young back then to look at it from every angle. Because I think that a man between 20 and 35 often is so busy living out his superficial sexuality that he has no time to deal with the finer points. He first lets off some steam, and only then does he realize that there was no place in his sex life for his personal erotic desires and individual inclinations.

That's how it was with me. It suddenly dawned on me, but how should I explain that to Ella? I knew she is a rather shy person and somewhat inhibited in bed. That doesn't mean that we only had sex in the dark back then. But she had never talked to me about her sexual desires and ideas openly and freely. She had never said to me on the spur of the moment: „*Let's try it this way today!*". She just wasn't the type. I was the one who showed her the ropes in bed. Therefore it was up to me to bring new sensual impulses into our relationship!

Ella: At the time we both felt subconsciously that something was happening to us. But the time still didn't seem right to say anything. But I noticed that you were giving me a certain look sometimes that evoked a very special feeling in me. Today I realize that your look already had that sexual authority at the time and that I was already longing to share your quite specific and in part rather bizarre ideas — I just didn't know it yet! I could never have imagined what was waiting for me ...

Hans: At sometime I decided to take a chance and gradually move your sexuality in the direction I had chosen for both of us: I wanted to dominate you sexually (at the time I didn't know that expression yet)! Because I knew it was the only way to reach new erotic horizons and in doing so save our relationship. I knew I had enough potential to be authoritarian, but what about you? I would find out ...

I had prepared everything well in advance. It was supposed to happen on our holidays, because I was sure it would be easier for you to lose your inhibitions in unfamiliar surroundings. We had taken a flight to Greece and had travelled from there to a small island; three wonderful weeks lay ahead of us there. We had gone during off-season and there were hardly any tourists left on the island. We had beautiful beaches and coves all to ourselves and I knew you would be able to relax there.

Before our departure I had bought various erotic *utensils*, and I was very anxious to see them in action. I didn't want my first *experiment* in sexual dominance to scare you off, that's why I picked something that focused on your pleasure. I had long wanted to drive you into a sexual frenzy and get you to experience multiple orgasms. So far you had always completely blocked off that possibility by withdrawing when I wanted to carry on after your first climax. This time, though, it wouldn't be up to you to decide, but I would direct your will!

After one week it already felt like paradise for both of us: long walks along the beach, swimming, snorkelling and endless sunshine! One evening we were sitting on the beach as the sun was setting and enjoying the enchanting atmosphere. Over the previous days I had made sure you were sexually *starved* so you would be good and ready. I began to fondle you, took off all your clothes and let you enjoy my caresses for a long time. You were writhing under my hands and lips and I soon noticed your growing desire. You were ready to abandon yourself to me and I knew: today was the day! Today I would *force* you to learn what's good for you, for us!

When your body was already twitching with sensual pleasure, when you were moaning and I could see the dark veil of ecstasy in your eyes, I turned you around on your belly. All too willingly you let it happen and even invitingly pushed out your hips towards me (that alone convinced me you had to be extremely aroused, otherwise you wouldn't have made that suggestive move!). Then I took a blindfold out of our beach bag and put it on you with the words: „*I want you to wear this now and do exactly what I tell you. Give yourself over to your desire, let yourself go – I'm here to catch you!*" Though you were very surprised, you were too excited to protest because now you wanted more and were longing to be satisfied! I guess the special atmosphere also played its part allowing you to completely relax.

When I began to explore your mounting desire with my hands you could hardly control yourself anymore. You wanted to turn around and face me again, but I gently forced you down again and ordered you to stay on your belly and lift your hips a little. Yes, that's how I wanted it. Exactly like that!

I now had perfect access to your genitals. Slowly I pulled the G-spot vibrator I had brought along out of the bag and turned it on. But I didn't stop indulging you with one hand. Softly humming, the toy set out to work, and in your boundless desire you didn't notice at first that the vibrator had taken the place of my finger now. It obviously did a good job because suddenly you began to jerk and contract rhythmically, wildly thrusting your whole lower body towards me and moaning louder than ever before. But that wasn't enough yet. I wanted more of your lust and simply carried on. While I was moving a little slower, I still didn't let you off the hook because I had a certain goal!

I grabbed your arm and turned you around so that you were lying on your back now. You were still blindfolded and completely out of breath — but still willing! I had long dreamed of this specific situation and made plans for realizing my dream. That day I would finally have my way thanks to my masculine authority and get you to come in a veritable chain of orgasms! To this end I had to dominate you sexually, i.e. make you do certain things by using physical and psychological pressure — certain gestures, words, orders, special rituals and treatments etc. Once I had checked out your reaction I wanted to gradually strengthen and extend this new relationship between us. In the meantime, after almost 10 years of sexual dominance, we have come to a point I can only call perfect in that sense. But first I should go on telling what happened at the beach in Greece back then:

I could see that the situation was too much for you; you didn't know whether you really should or could let it happen — but that's what I was there for! I took the decision away from you. When I went on caressing you and brought you closer and closer to another climax (but this time not only with my hands and the G-spot vibrator ...!), I experienced the full range of your lust for the first time. You were screaming with pleasure, writhing under me, completely immersed in another world, far removed from reality — in the world of our new sensual pleasures. And then it finally happened, you came again, explosively, in never ending waves, you were crying and laughing at the same time, and for the first time you had let yourself go completely ...

That was the beginning of a new relationship between us. In the meantime we have expanded our games, and to some extent I've become much harder in exercising my dominance than I was in the beginning. Whether I make you wait for me tied to the bed all day, make you blush with embarrassment (and flush other parts of your body at the same time) by threatening you with obscene promises in public or whether I force you to masturbate in the most shameless way before my lewd eyes — with your help I'm fulfilling my hottest erotic dreams simply by making sure they also become your dreams ...

The Art of Bondage and Flogging

Bondage Aids, Flogging Implements & Fetish Furniture

To practice what S/M fans call the *most beautiful ritual in the world*, namely erotic bondage games and voluntary exposure to torture, requires to know everything about the game. The active partner in particular should know the *rules of the game*. He should know exactly how to handle the aids and implements used to tie up his partner and how to quickly remove them in case the partner uses the previously determined code word in case of emergency. Compliance with this arrangement is an absolute must and is considered a prerequisite for any kind of erotic submission games, no matter if soft or hard.

The same goes for the use of whips or other flogging implements used in flagellation practices. Whoever thinks he could just *let fly* is hugely mistaken. Caning is an art that requires a lot of skill but also discipline and control — not only on the part of the passive partner. In addition, aesthetics play an important role here.

Below we will tell you about some of the best known and best suited bondage aids, flogging implements as well as fetish furniture (in some cases only available as a custom product) and explain their use as well as advantages and drawbacks:

Bondage Aids

Bondage aids are part of the standard product range of every well equipped sex shop. But many of the bondage utensils mentioned below can also be found in the household, that is they are normal consumer goods that are simply used for another purpose, namely to provide pleasure.

Handcuffs

At first glance handcuffs seem to be well suited for shackling since they are intended for this purpose. But that's not entirely true because handcuffs are only suitable for bondage games up to a point. For example, they are well suited to shackle the partner's hands to the bars of an iron bedstead. Many like the feel of the cold metal on their skin while others get a special sexual kick out of the fact that the very hard and inflexible material painfully cuts into their flesh. Basically, though, handcuffs are not suited for erotic bondage games because the possibilities for use are limited, not only concerning the duration of someone being shackled. Many S/M *experts* may prefer handcuffs, but for beginners and those who don't want to focus on pain but on the feeling of helplessness and powerlessness, handcuffs are too rigid and cold.

The Leather Strap

When using leather straps, the additional component of smell comes into play. Leather has something animalistic and its special scent can have a sexually arousing effect. But leather is a good material for bondage games even without its scent because it is soft and supple and quickly takes on body temperature. It is very important, though, to bear in mind that leather contracts with moisture (e.g. when used in the bathtub) and so can cut off the circulation of blood at the wrists, for example. One should also ensure that the knot isn't too tight, since otherwise the leather straps can only be undone with difficulty and may have to be cut, if necessary. If you still want to use this sensual natural product for your erotic bondage games, you should resort to purpose-made leather straps featuring buckles that can be opened and closed easily. They are available in any sex shop.

The Rope

The rope is the classic bondage implement. Despite of this it isn't particularly suited for erotic bondage games, since it often is very rough and hard, cuts into the flesh and can cause rope burns through friction when you move — which is hard to avoid in the throes of passion. Should you still decide on this means of bondage, the rope should be smooth, soft and made of natural fibre, if possible. Any kind of synthetic fibre feels unpleasant on the skin, generates warmth or even heat through friction and can therefore lead to rope burns. However, the rope has the advantage of being inexpensive and quick to hand.

The Belt

One of the true advantages of a belt is that one can be found in every household. It is also easy to handle because you can tie up your partner without necessarily having to tie a knot. It is better to use the buckle instead of a knot because it's easier to open again. Another advantage of the belt is its double function as bondage and flogging implement. If you want, you can use it for both purposes (see also flogging implements). However, the belt must be soft and supple. Plastic belts, for example, aren't suitable at all because they aren't flexible to the desired degree. A leather belt may also have a third function if the tied-up partner is additionally aroused by the scent of leather (osphresiolagnia).

The Scarf

When using a scarf for bondage games, the material is of primary importance. Thus, a silk scarf is better suited than one made of wool or synthetic fibres. However, it is difficult to open a knot with any material, especially if it was pulled too tight to begin with or if it tightens further through the movements of the tied-up partner. The advantage: almost everyone has a scarf at home so that you can indulge in bondage games on the spur of the moment!

The Silk Stocking

No matter if panty hose or silk stocking — the material is basically unsuitable for bondage games. The synthetic fibres easily cut into the skin of the tied-up partner. Still, panty hose are very popular since they are quick to hand and very flexible. However, if the knot is too tight, it is very hard to open and often must be cut, which destroys the panty hose and can easily lead to injuries! Any movement on the part of the tied-up partner also tends to further tighten the knot and cut off circulation. It's imperative to keep that in mind!

The Chain

The chain is only suitable for bondage if it is equipped with a hook at the end that replaces the knot. The cold, relatively inflexible material may be seen as an advantage or drawback, but for many that's exactly what makes up the appeal. The chain is a symbol for mercilessness and power because there is no way to break it. Once it is locked, it only opens when the dominant partner wants it to (or the shackled partner gives the signal/codeword in case of emergency). Basically the material doesn't feel very pleasant on the skin unless the shackled partner is crazy about metal.

The Wire

The use of a wire for bondage games should be avoided at all costs. While it is easy to close by twisting the ends, the material easily cuts into the skin and is relatively easy to bend so that the loop may open again. A wire leaves unsightly marks on the skin and its sharp ends may cause additional injuries — both to the *victim* and the *perpetrator*!

The Collar

Special fetishist collars — as well as all other bondage and torture implements mentioned below — are available in any good sex shop or as a custom made product. Collars come in a wide variety of form, colour and material and have the particular advantage of being specially made for the purpose of erotic bondage, i.e. they feature an easy to open and adjustable closing device (mostly buckles). They look good and emphasize the particular fetishist predilection of the user (e.g.

leather or latex, studs etc.). Furthermore, a chain can be attached to most collars allowing the submissive partner to be led on a leash like a dog. We advise against using animal collars on people.

The Thumbscrew

The thumbscrew is known as a pure instrument of torture (especially from the time of the inquisition). That it can also be used as an erotic aid lies in the nature of sadomasochism which uses pain and the infliction of pain to trigger sexual arousal. Only in very rare cases is the thumbscrew suitable for BD/SM games since it is aimed too much on purely inflicting pain. Basically it is more a part of the S/M scene but is mentioned here for the sake of completeness.

If someone wants to use thumbscrews as an erotic aid, it is imperative to talk about their use with the partner first. The level of pain inflicted must be carefully measured, too. Fixing the screws to the partner is often enough to cause sexual arousal without the need to tighten them. At any rate, this implement should be handled with the greatest care!

Reins and Bridle

In most cases this is a custom product made of leather. It is supposed to remind you of controlling a horse. In addition to the bridle, which is fitted to the neck or head of the submissive partner, there are also reins reaching down and enclosing the penis and testicles of a male submissive partner, allowing the dominant one even better control over his *horse.*

The Harness

The harness is reminiscent of the above mentioned bridle, though it has an additional wide leather strap that leads from the collar down to a garter belt where the hands can be fixed behind the back with the help of cuffs, severely restricting any movement on the part of the tied-up partner.

The Straitjacket

The straitjacket offers the possibility to render the submissive partner totally immobile from the waist up. Many bondage fans describe the process of being tied into a straitjacket as a complete turn on, since their arms and hands are completely immobile and fixed. In many cases additional bondage aids are used to tie up other parts of the body (for example ropes on the legs) and may even include fetish furniture (see below).

The Neck Iron

The neck iron is also a relic from the Middle Ages whose original purpose was to render an accused or condemned immobile so he could be punished. As the name implies, it is made of iron and is hinged so that the iron can be placed around the neck and closed again with a lock. It is not particularly suitable for erotic bondage games because it is heavy, cold and hard. A neck iron can cause injuries to the skin and can only be recommended if the submissive partner finds its medieval flair particularly appealing. Today, tough, one can also buy neck irons made of hard plastic, which greatly reduces the risk of injury.

Flogging Implements

A wide variety of special flogging implements like whips and paddles is available in any good sex shop. But there are also smaller specialty suppliers that carry particularly fine and unique specimens in their product range or specialize in custom manufacturing such fetish items. These aren't exactly cheap, of course!

The Whip

The whip is the classic flogging implement. However, there is a huge variety of whips which are almost always made of braided leather. Surely one of the best known is the *cat o' nine tails* which features a long grip and nine thick leather straps. There are special whips, for example, that have sharp-edged metal pieces embedded in the tips of the straps. If at all, they should only be used by true experts, because they can cause severe injuries and are intended more as a display of power than for actual use!

It takes some practice to have the whip land exactly where you want to stimulate the partner that needs to be punished. All in all there's not much to recommend the whip as an implement for flogging games, and if at all, then only for very soft lashes. The riding crop (see below), for example, is much more precise and easier to control.

The Riding Crop

The crop or riding crop is a long, firm rod made of braided leather. Its original purpose is to lead animals, espe-

cially horses. The greatest advantage of using a crop for flogging games is the possibility to place the strokes exactly
where you want to. With some practice the flagellator can
place the strokes (e.g. on the butt of the partner) side by side
with such precision that a fan-shaped pattern appears. The
purpose of this kind of flagellation is to stimulate the circulation of blood in the skin, causing a burning sensation. The
nerves lying directly below the skin are being stimulated by
the strokes, resulting in a strong sexual stimulus.

The Rod
The rod is well-suited for flogging games, first because
it is similar to the (riding) crop and shares its advantages (see
above), and secondly because it is easy to obtain. It can be
found everywhere in nature, which means that a stroll in the
woods is all that's needed to get another one and no money
needs to be reinvested if the rod is damaged or broken.

Especially popular and therefore recommendable is the
willow rod, since it is supple and very flexible while at the
same time being very tough.

The Belt
The belt is a rather practical flogging implement since
it is also suitable for bondage (double function), as mentioned
above. Furthermore it is quick to hand and quite inexpensive
compared to special whips or rods available in sex shops.
However, one drawback is that the belt doesn't have a grip
allowing a secure grasp and therefore must be wound around
the hand. This may result in the buckle pinching unpleasant-

ly. Moreover, its narrow and flat form doesn't allow for the same accuracy as a round crop. Even so, belts are very popular for flogging games since they remind you of being punished by your father.

The Cane

The cane is especially popular with fans of so-called caning games, since it is reminiscent of being punished by a strict teacher or governess. It is not as elastic and flexible as a crop, but a little thicker and stiffer. It also allows for a good aim at the body parts you want to hit. However, strokes with the cane may be more painful than those with a crop because the cane is harder. So care must be taken!

The Paddle

The paddle differs from the rod in that its hitting surface is wide and flat and its handle is shorter. The paddle, too, is most often made of (very thick) leather, whereby several layers are glued or stitched together. Using a paddle allows you to stimulate larger areas of skin at once without running the risk of cutting into the skin, as can easily happen when using a whip.

Paddles come in a wide variety, too, and not only differ in colour and form, but there are also extreme models that are studded. However, such paddles should only be used by flogging experts, since one must consider the risk of injury here, too. Paddles are available in any good sex shop or S/M specialty stores.

The Stick

While the stick may be the simplest implement for flogging games, it still can't be recommended for this use. It is completely stiff and most often far too thick and hard. The lack of flexibility makes it impossible to judge the intensity of the strokes. The risk of injury — especially to the joints and bones of the partner being flagellated — is very high!

Fetish Furniture

Special fetish furniture is not available in normal furniture stores. For the most part it is custom made, in some cases to the exact body measurements and specifications of the customer. Most often a carpenter is asked to custom manufacture the pieces, or the sexy furniture can be obtained from specialized dealers of fetish furniture or other suppliers in the S/M scene. One thing is true for all pieces of fetish furniture: they cost more than a normal chair or an ordinary commercially available bed!

St. Andrew's Cross

A St. Andrew's cross is shaped like an X (so-called diagonal cross) and is made of a massive material, usually wood. It is equipped with strong leather straps at the ends of the beams to tie up the submissive partner. Thus fixed to the cross, one can endure the attentions of the dominant partner for hours in relative comfort with legs that are inevitably widely spread.

By the way, the St. Andrew's cross owes its name to the apostle Andrew who is supposed to have died on such a cross.

The Love Swing

Like any normal swing, the love swing is also attached to the ceiling or a beam by means of hooks and chains/ropes. Down below, the four ropes wind up in a meshwork of plastic or leather straps that are attached to each other so you can easily climb into it with your (usually bare) butt and place the legs in such a way that you are hanging over the floor in a somewhat tilted position. You can swing in any direction. If constructed properly, the love swing allows for a comfortable suspension. The partner can control the direction and intensity of the swinging motion.

The Rack

The rack, too, was used in the Middle Ages for torture. It is equipped with various devices, cogs and mechanisms to stretch the person fixed to the rack and thus inflict pain. Any racks available today are usually custom made (for S/M studios) and are of course much more *luxurious* than 500 years ago, since fortunately today's purpose of the rack is no longer a merciless death through torture, but sexual arousal through pain. Still, caution is imperative, because the partner fixed to the rack can easily be harmed physically!

The Spanking Bench

The spanking bench is reminiscent of a gymnastics apparatus, the only difference being that it features additional loops for fixation. It is a four-legged massive wooden trestle (usually covered in leather) and about as high as a chair. The submissive partner bends over it and is tied on hands and feet. There are various ways of using the spanking bench. The bound partner can stand up and bend over the bench or lie flat on the bench with her/his whole body.

Final Comments

Surely you may find one or the other *confession* of our interviewees more appealing than another, inspiring your fantasy to frivolous flights of fancy which you may want turn into reality one day; or perhaps some of the reports shocked you so much that you can't imagine going through that experience under any circumstances. Not everyone has a customized St. Andrew's cross made for him which he then sets up in the bedroom for pleasurable use. And not every woman is crazy about feeling the prickle of tender lashes on her butt. On the other hand, it's certainly not wrong to expand one's own sexual horizon, to be open for something new and to inform oneself about various erotic aids. When it comes to BD/SM in particular, there are no limits to the imagination, and sooner or later titillating ideas like bondage or caning, for example, enter the rituals. If, how, how hard or how often this happens is an entirely personal decision. What is important is to create the right conditions.

And that's precisely the aim of this book: it is not designed to highlight very special, extremely bizarre fetishist practices in minute detail, but to give the reader a chance to get a *taste* of the subject. It is supposed to inform him about the possibilities of BD/SM in a partnership and tease out any sexual proclivities that may already exist in the reader; it is meant to define the boundaries of shame already during the reading, to stimulate your fantasy and to show ways of living out this extremely juicy and diverse game with the aid of concrete examples of *S/M experts.* Our interviewees show you what it could be like; you decide for yourself what it actually is like when you wake the *sleeping dragon* in yourself and your partner!

Of course BD/SM is not a must, and it's rules and rituals are not meant for every partnership. If you read this book and decide for yourself: „*That's not for me; that goes far beyond what I could ever do*", then this doesn't mean you are a *sexual bore* by a long shot! The diversity in the area of eroticism is huge, and the enormous selection surely offers something for everyone. To get a little taste of this and that and find out what practices definitely suit you, what you might like and what puts you off can only be recommended!

I hope this book will help you uncover more of your sensual potential and encourage you to try out BD/SM games. The fact that this subject already has attracted your attention is proof enough that BD/SM could also give your partnership the final kick of pleasure. If you (and certain parts of your body!) are itching to try out this game – do it!

Ina Stein

Sexuality is not a self-contained
part of human life.
It is a ray permeating
every human relationship,
but shining with particular intensity in certain places.

(ALAN W. WATH, RELIGIOUS PHILOSOPHER)

ANAL SEX

Kim Powers

Turning HER on to ANAL-SEX

Non-Fiction

Turning HER on to ANAL-SEX

Prickly desire for anal experiences? Then this is just right for you! This book is chock full of concrete tips, utterly frank firsthand reports and detailed instructions all around the subject of anal sex. Because women, especially, often feel quite insecure and may even be afraid when her partner wants to introduce her to anal eroticism. That's why this book is the optimal aide for HER and HIM. We show you step by step how she, too, can become an enthusiastic »Analita«, because here men can find out how to turn their partner on to anal games.

We offer you informal information, give important safety pointers, present an overview of a great variety of anal toys and most of all: men and women talk about their first anal experiences with complete frankness here, reporting about the full range of their anal adventures. Whether anal slip, bead chain or anal plug – there are many possibilities to experience ecstasy with »Greek love«, and a woman can indulge her man »through the backdoor«, too …

This book will leave HER and HIM wanting MORE!

0130346 0000 • 112 9ages   ISBN 3-7986-0180-1

By: Kim Powers

How to dominate HIM

Becoming a perfect
DOMINATRIX

Non-Fiction

How to dominate HIM
Becoming a perfect DOMINATRIX

… her long red fingernails leaving visible marks on his skin, which he will feel for a long time yet and will always remind him of the feeling of boundless horniness. He is lying on his back, his hands fixed above to the metal bedstead, his ankles restrained in the same way. He is helpless – and loves being at the mercy of his beautiful mistress! She is playing with his lust, turning him on more and more …

Many men dream of being treated like a slave by their dominant partner in bed and of submitting to her kinky desires. Fittingly, women also have lustful S/M fantasies: they would like to slip into the role of the strict dominatrix and spoil their partner with sweet torments. In this book we will show you the ropes of this exciting game of dominance and submission and what makes a perfect dominatrix. We will introduce you to special S/M techniques and implements, kinky fetish wear and furniture, after which we will abduct you into the world of perverse firsthand reports and hot book excerpts we selected for you.

Conclusion: Put your will into her strict hands and she will teach you the pleasure of pain!

0130354 0000 • 128 pages   ISBN 3-7986-0183-6